Introduction to
PYROGRAPHY

For Georgi

Introduction to
PYROGRAPHY
THE ART OF WOODBURNING

Daniel Wright

SEARCH PRESS

First published in Great Britain 2004

Search Press Limited
Wellwood, North Farm Road,
Tunbridge Wells, Kent TN2 3DR

Text copyright © Daniel Wright 2004

Photography by Charlotte de la Bédoyère, Search Press Studios

ISBN 1 903975 37 9

The Publishers and author can accept no responsibility for any consequences arising from the information, advice or instructions given in this publication.

Thanks and acknowledgements are due to a number of people, without whose help publication would not have been possible. These include:

the team at Search Press
Janik Ltd.
Peter Child Woodturning Supplies
The Craftsman magazine
Albert Lain and all at Finewood
Dawn Stanton
Alun Scarlett
Mike Arbon
Rachael Lowe
Bob Neil
Norman Hawkes
Georgiana Hawkes
Richard Withers
all the artists who have provided me with inspiration to produce my work
and most importantly my parents for their tremendous support.

Publisher's note

All the step-by-step photographs in this book feature the author, Daniel Wright, demonstrating pyrography. No models have been used.

Page 1
An intricate Celtic knot design worked on a shallow lime bowl

Page 2
A dwarf with all his worldly goods – the lid of a lime pencil box

Page 3
Fruit-shaped boxes worked with a variety of different designs

Page 4
Fairy design on an apple turned in lime wood

Page 5
A dragon design worked on the top of a stool – see page 44 to see the complete design

Printed in Malaysia by Times Offset (M) Sdn Bhd

CONTENTS

INTRODUCTION

For every art and craft medium, there is a wide range of different, but equally appropriate techniques. In pyrography, just as in watercolour or ceramics, no one way is correct. This becomes evident when you look at the work of professional pyrographers: not only does the work reflect the style of the artist, it also demonstrates the use of many individual techniques developed over the years, whether through endeavour or happy chance. Experience shows when to apply these techniques to suit the materials available or the subject matter.

My first experience of pyrography was as a child on a family holiday in North Wales. After a week of incessant rain, my family sought refuge in a craft centre at Corris, where I met professional pyrographer Richard Withers. The walls of his unit were lined with dynamic, flamboyant work, and I knew that it was what I wanted to do. At first my parents were unconvinced, but before the end of the week their resistance had weakened and I persuaded them that someone should benefit from the washout of a holiday. I left Wales armed with my first machine – which I later discovered was manufactured just down the road from my home in Suffolk – and a few pearls of pyrographic wisdom which have proved invaluable:

- Certain woods work better than others for pyrographic work: do not use cheap softwoods. Light-coloured hardwoods are best for beginners.
- Always keep a piece of scrap wood to use in much the same way as an artist uses a sketchbook, to avoid making mistakes on an expensive piece of wood.
- A machine which resembles a pen is easier to grasp and control. You cannot expect to produce fine, detailed work with a cumbersome, hard-to-control poker tool.

Given my tender age when I began, and the predisposition of most ten-year-olds towards fads, it would not have been surprising if, after a few initial fumblings, the machine had been left to gather dust. Though it was some years before I felt I was in control of the machine rather than vice versa, persistence pays relatively fast dividends in pyrography. In the absence of a teacher I developed my own techniques, borrowing from a range of fine art practices including pen-and-ink, engraving and watercolour. Within a short time, I was selling my work and soon afterwards, instructing others. A word of advice: if you use other people's work to inspire you, make sure you understand the copyright laws and, in any case, do not copy too slavishly or your work will lack spontaneity.

For the would-be pyrographer drawing ability is useful but by no means essential. Crude work is often very effective in this medium, something I first noted when running workshops with children. It is often not the most gifted artists who produce the best work. The purpose of this book is not to dissect all possible pyrography techniques, but rather to explain how and why I make the choices I do. I hope this will give the beginner following my guidelines a head start, and that even a seasoned professional may be able to pick up fresh ideas.

Opposite
A walnut bowl returns to its
roots – see pages 58-61

History

As soon as you begin to experiment with pyrography, you notice it all around you. In a more primitive form, the craft has been practised for millennia, and examples can be found in the art of most cultures.

No one knows exactly how old pyrography is, but early examples include a cup decorated with humming birds excavated from a Nazca settlement in Peru. This cup has been dated to before 700 A.D. Evidence of pyrography unearthed on Roman sites in Britain include a decorated caudex, which is the woody stem-cover found on some perennials. Traditionally, pyrography was used to decorate everyday items like wooden spoons or drinking horns, which is why little evidence is left today.

Wood-burning began to be seen as an art form rather than a folk craft in medieval Europe. The artist and engraver Albrecht Dürer is known to have practised it, and it is

claimed that the painters Rembrandt and Brouwer used it to decorate the wainscoting of their local taverns. In Britain, it can be seen as poker-work graffiti on Tudor beams and it complements marquetry on 18th-century furniture. More recently the writer Victor Hugo and the artist Picasso dabbled with the craft.

Throughout the 17th and 18th centuries, professional pyrographers were employed to decorate ornate furniture, but it was not until the Victorian era that pyrography became established in the public realm, and was used to decorate a wide range of household items. With the growth of the Arts and Crafts movement, magazines encouraged middle-class ladies of leisure to put down their needlework and pursue pyrography as a hobby and for profit. Evidence shows that it was not the most genteel of pastimes. Advances in technology meant that people no longer had to burn pictures with red-hot pokers straight out of a coal burner. The latest machine to be developed involved pumping benzene, a highly inflammable substance, to heat the nib. It meant that a constant temperature could be maintained, but the practitioner had to operate bellows to pump the benzene with one hand while working with the other. The risk to life posed by the dangerous cocktail of ingredients and working methods must have been considerable.

Electricity began to be used for pyrography in the 20th Century. Initially, the tools were modelled on soldering irons, and it was not until the early 1970s that manufacturers perfected the machines used by the majority of pyrographers today. These machines were designed specifically for ease of use, which gave the pyrographer infinitely more control and precision than was possible before.

Pyrography is in a unique position: while it is one of the most ancient crafts, the recent technological advances mean that it is also in its infancy. Its potential has been revolutionised, and pyrographers are only beginning to explore its possibilities. In another thirty years, pyrography may achieve a more prominent status in the world of craft, or even art.

Daniel Wright.

Above
Elephant money box – detail

This circus scene is based on an old illustration and pyrographed on the lid of an old box for an antique feel. See page 82 for more information.

Opposite
Pyrography can be used to enhance old and new items of all shapes and sizes.

MATERIALS

When I am at craft fairs, I often speak to people who have tried pyrography without much success and have subsequently given up. This is usually due to their choice of machine, which invariably turns out to be a simple poker tool not unlike a soldering iron. The only advantage I can see to these tools is their cheapness, which is the reason that many beginners opt for them. But poker tools are difficult to use and clumsy: imagine trying to draw while holding a pencil a long way from its tip. These tools tend to become hot through the tip, and have no temperature control.

Pyrography machines

There are machines on the market that are specifically designed for pyrography, and are a far better choice for the beginner than a simple poker tool. The extra cost will pay dividends very quickly.

Solid point machine

This is less expensive than the hot wire machine and offers a range of decorative possibilities. It is a good choice for patterned work, but less good for artistic realism. This machine is useful for producing bold, design-based pyrography, and the branding technique can be used to complement most work. A drawback is that the points are not immediately responsive, and it is difficult to achieve tonal range. A number of differently-shaped screw-in nibs are available, including needle points for line work, flat nibs for blocking in and a range of different nibs for branding.

Hot wire machine

This is the choice for the majority of professionals, and is what I use myself. It is also the best choice if you want to attempt the exercises in this book. The cost of the machine is the biggest outlay when you begin pyrography, but I think it is worth paying a little more for a hot wire machine. In this case, the nib is a piece of flexible wire, and the effect is more subtle. The heat can be controlled and the pen itself is very responsive, creating more opportunity for tonal depth and fine detail. Different nibs are available, but I find a spoon-point is suitable for most purposes.

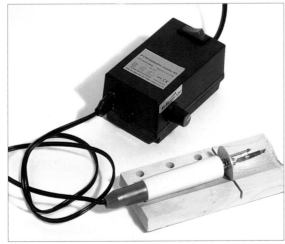

Solid-point machines like these are best-sellers

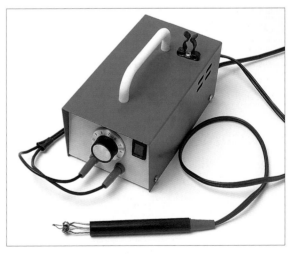

The hot wire pyrography machine I use

Opposite
A wide variety of wood
and leather blanks are available

Wood

The quality of the work you produce will always be governed by your choice of wood. This is not a problem as long as your design matches the pyrographic qualities of the wood chosen. The nature of wood, and the fact that the pieces will always vary, mean that it is impossible to make absolute distinctions between the different types. Here is a list of general guidelines:

• Make sure that the surface you are working is as smooth as possible. Sand the wood thoroughly with the grain, using different grades of sandpaper from coarse through to fine.

• Beginners can easily find good, cheap sources of wood to practise on: items like spoons, spatulas and bread boards can be picked up very cheaply from kitchen reject shops. These are usually made from *beech*. This is a useful wood: the grain can be quite defined so line pictures work well. These kitchen objects are usually left unfinished: take care not to buy wood that has been varnished or lacquered.

• Plywood, which is cheap and is often faced in *birch*, is another ideal wood for beginners.

• Light hardwoods such as *sycamore, lime, holly* and *maple* are the most frequently used. Their pale colour offers the greatest contrast to the work, and their grain is less troublesome. I also enjoy using wood from fruit trees like *pear* and *cherry.*

• *Yew, walnut* and *ash* are all useful woods, and offer a more beautiful 'canvas' to work on than the plain white woods, but the unpredictable nature of the grain means that you must adjust your expectations accordingly, and opt for bolder designs with little or no tonal variation. Darker woods such as *rosewood* or *teak* are worth experimenting with.

• *Oak, elm* and soft conifers like *pine* can be used, but only on a very simple level. Their grains are very disruptive and make the pyrography nib burn unevenly. Dark woods like *mahogany* will rarely complement your work, unless you are seeking a very subtle effect.

• There may be times when you will be reluctant to try to improve on nature. Beautifully-grained woods such as *lacewood* and *satinwood* are very responsive, but they may be best left alone.

A selection of woods that can be used for pyrography, shown in their natural state

Beech

Birch

Sycamore

Pear

Cherry

African Black Walnut

Ash

Rosewood

Horse Chestnut

Teak

Pine

Oak

Lime

Elm

Satinwood

Equipment

After the initial outlay on a machine, pyrography is an inexpensive hobby to pursue. You will probably already own most of the equipment required to plan your work, practise the craft successfully and maintain your machine:

Pencil

Use this for initial planning of designs and to transfer them to your wood before you start burning. A medium pencil (HB) is ideal on light woods, but a fairly soft pencil (2B) will show up more clearly on dark woods and leather.

Pencil sharpener

Keep your pencil sharp so you can produce intricate designs, in order to generate the very fine detail of which your machine is capable.

Eraser

Use this when planning designs, and to remove pencil marks from wood after burning. Erasing pencil marks will make your work look neater, and may also reveal areas you have missed with your pyrography pen.

Coloured pencils

Packs of pencils designed to imitate skin tones are useful for reproducing the range of brown tones that can be created by wood-burning. They are ideal for building up preparatory sketches with the appropriate coloration to be used as a blueprint for your work.

Compasses

Use these when planning designs such as circular borders.

Ruler

This is sometimes used to create straight edges to your designs, and also to measure designs or map out patterns.

Pens

I use pens with nibs of various sizes to work preparatory sketches.

Tracing paper

This is used to transfer your designs on to your wood.

Carbon paper

This can also be used to transfer designs to your wood. If you place carbon paper on your wood with a drawing on top, you can simply trace the outlines and the carbon paper will mark your designs on the wood.

Sandpaper

This is an essential tool in your armoury. It is used to prepare wood to take a picture: the smoother the surface, the better it will be to work on. It may also be used to sand away small mistakes while working. When a piece is finished, use it to sand back the edges of objects, which may have become discoloured by the natural oils in your hands.

Adhesive tape

Use this to fix down carbon paper or tracing paper when transferring designs.

Emery paper

This is useful for sanding away small areas of a picture to expose lighter wood, and give greater tonal impact to your pyrography. Do not use it to prepare wood, as it will leave a rough finish. Buy fine grade.

My box of essential equipment

Scissors

Use these to cut emery paper into small pieces for easy handling.

Wire

This can be cut to size and used to form replacement nibs for hot-wire machines. As an alternative, you can buy ready-made nibs from the machine's manufacturer.

Screwdriver

Use this to maintain your hot-wire machine and to change nibs.

Multi-purpose tool

These are useful for everything from fixing on key-ring attachments to scraping gourds.

TECHNIQUES

I frequently run workshops for people who are attempting pyrography for the first time, and find that they are rarely disappointed with their results. With care, beginners can produce extremely accomplished work. The achievement of gaining full control over your pyrography equipment and its capabilities may take a lot longer.

The key to skilful pyrography is being in command of the pen – regardless of the differing characteristics of different surfaces – and being able to direct precisely the lines and marks you make, rather than having to adjust your design to account for happy or unhappy accidents. The best way to make the transition from beginner to skilled practitioner is with lots of practice.

A good rule to follow is to start small and gradually broaden your ambitions. This will help you to build up confidence, and become familiar with your equipment. I started on spoons and spatulas, working line drawings with no variation in tone but using shadings to add texture and depth. Key-rings, egg-cups and other small items are also suitable. Plywood templates cut to resemble animals or other familiar shapes are available from pyrography suppliers. These provide the outline, so all you have to do is fill in the details. All these items are inexpensive, so you need not risk costly mistakes. If a piece goes badly wrong, it is better to throw away a key-ring than a clock. Working small also means that you can learn in bite-size chunks.

Holding the pyrography tool

Here are some useful hints on method and adapting what you already know about using conventional drawing implements to pyrography:

• Hold the pyrography pen just as you would any other writing or sketching implement. The pen should feel well-balanced: keep your hand as near to the nib as possible for maximum control.

• For most types of wood, the heat control should be set at a level just below the temperature needed to make the nib – or coil, if you use a solid-point machine – glow perceptibly red. Certain woods will require more heat; gourds, leather and delicate pieces may need less heat. If you use too much heat, the result will be overburn, an unsightly orange scorching around your lines. This usually occurs when impatient pyrographers turn the heat too high to work quicker. Full power is seldom needed.

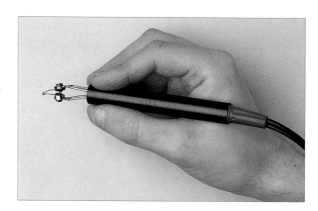

• Using your pyrography pen is similar to using a pencil, through far slower. Take care not to apply pressure: you should simply be burning the surface. Just touch the surface of the wood and work very slowly to allow it time to burn. If you push downwards, you will gouge the wood. It will be apparent when you have grasped the initial technique because your lines will be crisp, and of an even thickness and colour.

Shading

Pyrography has parallels with other artistic techniques, and it can be used to imitate drawing, painting and etching styles. The examples right demonstrate the range of tone that can be achieved by varying speed of stroke and temperature. Start with a medium heat setting and increase it if necessary.

While you are building your confidence and becoming accustomed to the machine, it is a good idea to disregard its tonal capabilities and learn to build up pictures with lines of one tone. An ideal way to do this is to attempt to mimic the mark-making and drawing style of pen and ink. Pen-and-ink work is uniform in tone, but uses hatchings and contrast between dark and light to suggest tonal variation.

Monotone pyrography relies on the fact that wood will only burn so dark. For the best results, take your time when you are producing dark lines: beginners, used to the speed at which ordinary pens form marks, invariably work far too quickly. The result is uneven work that looks washed-out. If you are trying to achieve maximum darkness, it will not matter if you burn some areas more than others as they will appear equally dark. On a wood that does not burn consistently, lighter tonal work may look blotchy, but if you work to achieve maximum burn it will look uniform in tone.

Light shading

To achieve this effect, use a spoon-point nib and keep it moving evenly over your work. Make sure that your temperature control is not set too high.

Dark shading

Move the nib more slowly to achieve this effect, and go over the area more than once if necessary.

Creating tone

To **lighten the intensity of tone** lower the heat control on your machine.

To **darken the tone of your line**, slow down the speed of your stroke. This gives the wood more time to burn so it becomes darker. Lines can be darkened in mid-flow: for example, if you want your work to darken gradually towards a certain area, slow the speed of your stroke progressively as you approach it.

To **broaden your line and make it darker**, apply a little extra downward pressure on your nib at the relevant point in your design. Remember that you should never apply much pressure: generally, the nib should just touch the wood.

Starting small

For your first projects, you might prefer to work on smaller items. These inexpensive ready-made pieces are ideal while you are building up your confidence and learning the techniques in this book.

This pen and ink design, prepared for a wedding invitation, could work equally well as a woodburning.

Silhouettes

Silhouette relies upon creating an outline of a picture, then filling in the area inside. The technique is simple, so silhouettes are ideal first projects for people new to the craft of pyrography. Even a complete beginner will be able to produce highly decorative and competent-looking work.

Silhouettes work best if the design is exaggerated: think of the art of silhouette portraiture, where noses and foreheads protrude to make the likeness more angular, and therefore more interesting. Accurate outlines are important for good results, so choose designs with clear edges. Books of silhouettes crammed with expert examples are available, skilfully devised to show subjects from the best angle for this purpose. Portraits, unless they are in profile, are not suitable. If you have chosen this technique because the surface is difficult to work on, perhaps because your wood does not burn evenly so needs to be worked in monochrome, make sure your design is not too fiddly or your edges may become blurred.

To begin, trace or sketch the outlines of a picture on to a piece of wood using a soft pencil, then follow the lines with your pyrographic pen, using a standard nib for accuracy. To change direction, you may find it easier to turn the wood, rather than the pen nib. When the outline is complete, block in the area it contains using a standard point on a high heat (see page 27), taking care not to go over any edges.

Any areas which have not achieved the ideal matt, almost-black tone when your work is complete can be reworked if necessary using a higher heat setting.

Romeo and Juliet

These silhouetted figures against a line-drawn background may provide you with inspiration.

> ## Note
>
> Carbon paper can be used to transfer designs to wood. Place the carbon paper on the wood with a drawing on top and simply trace the outlines to mark out your designs.

Opposite
Silhouette plaque

This picture is adapted from an Arthur Rackham illustration for the fairy tale Sleeping Beauty. An area has been left blank for a name to transform it into a plaque for the door of a child's room.

Reverse silhouette

The trees on the plaque shown opposite are worked from simple sketches and created using a form of reverse silhouette, in which the area outside the outline is filled in. I have added sketchy details to the tree shapes to indicate foliage.

There is a profusion of Victorian poker-work to be found in antique shops, and most of this uses silhouette and reverse silhouette. Magazines and books of that era included pattern sheets of such designs, which, given the crudeness of the methods used, is not surprising. Even though tools are now more advanced, this technique is still the easiest route to successful and pleasing results. You have seen how some woods work better than others, but if you find yourself working on a difficult surface, where grain will interrupt line, and mid-tones cannot effectively be achieved, silhouette will always enable you to produce fine work.

The examples on these pages here have much in common with the border projects on pages 30-37, which are also forms of reverse silhouette. When you are creating your own designs, think about the balance of dark and light and experiment with the look of different proportions of these.

Tree sampler

This piece on sycamore wood was adapted from an illustration on tree identification by Adrian Hill to produce a crib-sheet of trees and their Latin names. You can keep pieces individual by randomly selecting an assortment of these trees when starting a new piece.

The illustration below demonstrates how you may create your own tree motifs. I made a quick sketch, then adapted it first into a silhouette and then a reverse silhouette.

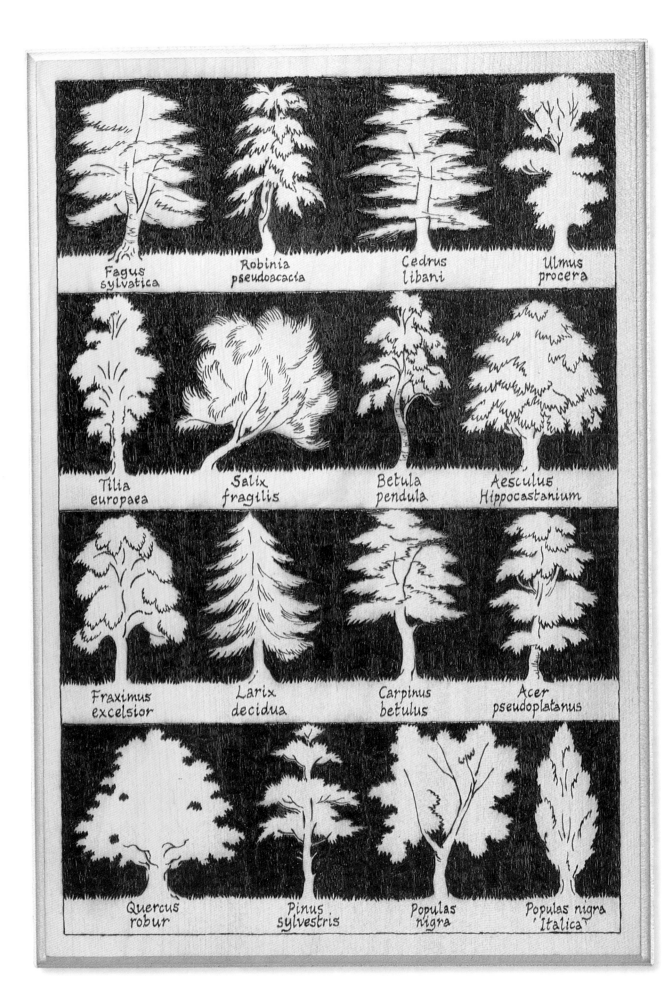

Project
Tree vase

This project is particularly suited to curved surfaces. Turned vases such as the one shown, which has a pronounced curve, can be a challenge. Yet, with a simple design, most shapes can be tackled. A design may be adapted to go around a bowl or any turned piece.

Before you begin, consider your layout. This is a matter of personal choice, but a little time spent planning the effect you wish to achieve could help you to avoid a disappointing result. Measure the circumference and work out how many trees you should place for best effect. I have used eleven examples of trees around this vase, meaning that three trees can be seen when it is viewed from the side. If I had made the band deeper each tree would have been correspondingly broader so fewer would have been needed to circle the vase. This might have meant that only two trees would have been seen when viewed from the side. If I had made the band shallower and therefore included more trees, I might have risked losing detail or impact.

Another question to consider is whether to locate the band at the top of your object, at the bottom, or centrally as I have done. When you have made your choices, use light pencil marks to plan the design on your object before you begin to work it. Alternatively, you can cut a band of tracing paper, work out your tree design flat, then wrap it round the vase and transfer the design. This is relatively easy because the curve on this vase is so slight.

You will need

Elm vase

Pencil

Eraser

Pyrography tool

Spoon-point nib

Broader nib if desired –
see step 3

1. Sketch your design on the vase using light pencil marks so you can erase them if necessary, then follow the pencil lines with your pyrography tool. Make sure the heat is set high enough to create a consistently dark line. Tilt the object as you work so you do not have to contort your arm uncomfortably.

Tip

To pencil a border on a circular object, stand it next to a stack of books built up to just below the height you want your line. Hold a pencil firmly on top of the stack so the point just touches the object. Rotate the object to draw the straight line.

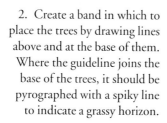

2. Create a band in which to place the trees by drawing lines above and at the base of them. Where the guideline joins the base of the trees, it should be pyrographed with a spiky line to indicate a grassy horizon.

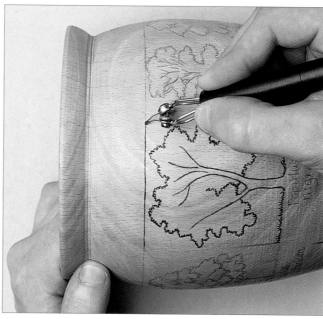

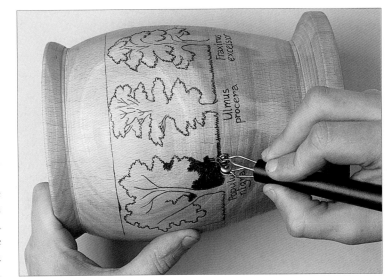

3. When the lines are in place, begin to block in the 'negative space'. Where possible, this should be done uniformly with horizontal strokes across the grain, which produces a darker effect than working with the grain. For speed, you can use a broader nib.

The finished vase

The tree outlines are not reverse silhouettes in the truest sense because some detail has been added within the outlines. Using this technique allows you the freedom to add as much or as little detail as you wish.

Basic patterns

These examples demonstrate the range of nibs you will need to undertake the chessboard project.

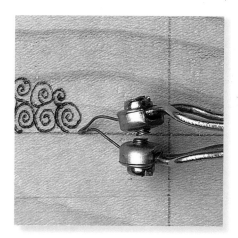

Standard nib

This nib is useful for a range of pyrography techniques, and is the most practical nib to use when you want to create flowing lines. Work from the inside of each swirl, radiating outwards. Fill in the square with swirls of random sizes, working the swirls both clockwise and anti-clockwise.

Swirls

Spoon-point nib

Use the bowl of a spoon-point nib on a high heat, leaving areas of wood untouched between each dot. For even circles, make sure that the bowl of the nib makes contact at the correct angle; it should be exactly parallel to the surface.

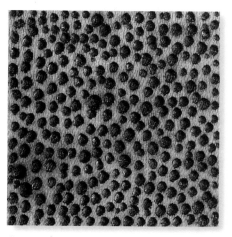

Large dots

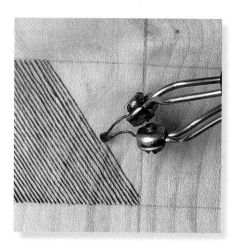

Inverted spoon-point

To produce the finest lines, invert the spoon-point so you are working with the edge. You will need to work freehand, but the cutting nature of the nib will keep your lines surprisingly straight. Work up to the pencil boundaries but try to avoid blotches where lines start and finish.

Fine lines

Project
Chessboard

This project adapts a traditional 'tester' method of exploring pyrography to produce a functional and attractive object. A tester is typically a flat board, divided into squares, with a different shading technique filling each square. Most pyrographers have completed at least one, if not many, in their wood-burning career. It is a valuable exercise as pyrography relies solely on using a range of marks to build up pictures. Students of etching undertake similar testers as a foundation stone of their training.

The following pages show some of the different techniques I used to fill my tester, and instructions on how to achieve similar effects. You may wish to experiment with your own. The finished chessboard tester will be a useful resource, to which you will return again and again when deciding exactly how to enliven your line drawings. Basic pictures can be built up just using line and outline, but it is not until you add shadings that your work comes to life.

Planning and executing the project

You will need a large piece of wood, preferably light hardwood. Prepare the surface by sanding it lightly (see page 12). Mark out the largest square possible on the wood, using a unit of measurement that will divide easily by ten, for example 30cm^2; 40cm^2 or a measurement in inches. I used 30cm^2. Divide adjacent sides of your square by ten and mark with a pencil. Join up the marks to create a grid of 100 squares.

Disregard the outermost 36 squares, which will be used to form the border, and work on the inner 64 squares. Half of these should be filled like a chequer board. Try to shade each of the squares using a different method, exploring as many different nibs or pen inserts as you have with your machine. Work up to the edges of each square so that the shadings delineate the squares, rather than outlining them physically.

You will need

A large piece of wood

Ruler

Set square

Pencil

Eraser

Pyrography tool

An assortment of nibs

The completed chessboard

Instructions for completing the border begin on page 32

Loose weave

Use a standard nib to create random groups of lines: blocks of three or four short parallel lines, drawn in all directions so they meet without gaps. This texture is useful for backgrounds.

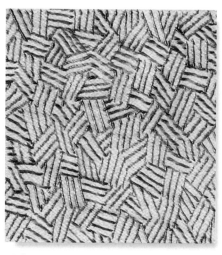

Tight weave

Work in the same way as for loose weave, but leave smaller spaces between each parallel line. These weave shadings create interesting backgrounds for pictures.

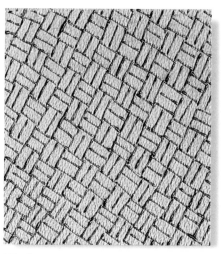

Block weave

Use a standard nib to create uniform blocks of three parallel lines. This texture can be used to imitate sacking.

Herringbone

Use a standard point to build up the lines as shown. This technique can be used to give the impression of depth, and shows the potential of pyrography for creating optical illusions.

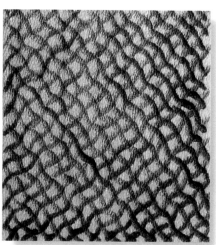

Mesh

Use the bowl of a spoon-point for this technique, which can be achieved by making a rhythmic rocking movement of the hand while drawing a line. The lines do not exactly echo one another, but should be roughly equidistant.

Heavy wave

Use a spoon point and start at the bottom right-hand corner with a waving line. Each subsequent line should be roughly equidistant, and should follow the wave of the previous line. I have often used this shading to suggest ploughed fields.

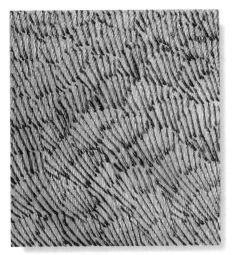

Shell pattern

Use a standard point to create hatchings that radiate outwards in clusters. This is the shading I would normally use to represent foliage, especially trees.

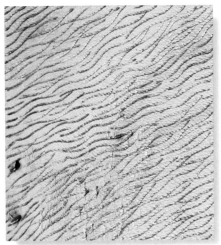

Streaky wood grain

Use the standard nib to build up wavy lines that cross one another at intervals. This technique produces a subtle wood grain and may also be used to suggest moving water.

Wood grain with knots

Use the standard point to put in the oval knots randomly, then add the rest of the lines radiating from them. This is a useful, slightly humorous way, to suggest the appearance of wood grain.

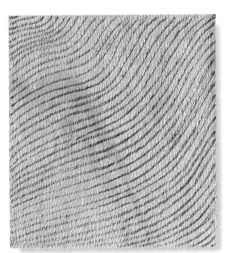

Fine wave

Use the standard point and work in exactly the same way as for the heavy wave. This technique shows how shadings can create movement and depth and is good for creating recession in a picture.

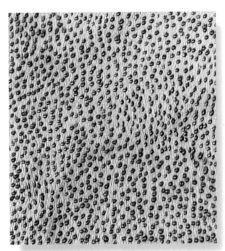

Small dots

These are similar to large dots but are created using a standard point so it takes far longer to fill the square. Some pyrographers use this pointillist approach for all their work. This texture is good for landscape work.

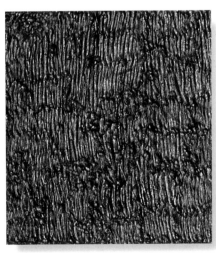

Dark effect

Use a standard point on a high heat to block in the square. The finer point creates more ridges for the light to catch so the overall effect is very different from the dark square created with the spoon-point nib (see page 17). Use this texture for blocking in around reverse silhouette work.

 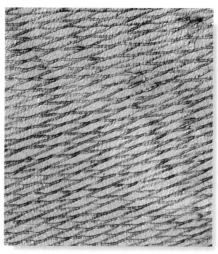

Mixed shading

Use the bowl of the spoon-point nib to put in an under-layer of even, light shading. Use the standard nib to add the upper, staccato shading.

Slanted cross-hatch

Use the inverted spoon-point nib to create interesting surfaces by cross-hatching uniformly, but not at right angles. Use this shading in combination with other crosshatch variations to build up varying planes of background.

Slanted cross-hatch 2

Again using the inverted spoon-point nib, this variation of the previous technique shows how to vary the effect by changing the angle at which two hatchings bisect.

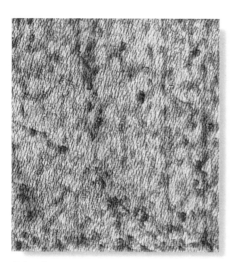  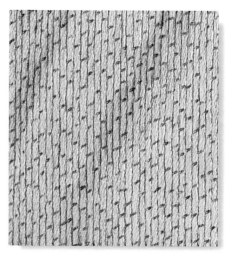

Stippling

Use the bowl of a spoon-point on a high heat to fill the surface with a scribbling motion in random directions. This is a good choice for creating backgrounds.

Standard cross-hatch

Use the spoon-point nib inverted to draw fine lines. The hatchings are uniform, and cross at right angles. Note that the 'waves' seen in this example are just the grain of the wood.

Cellular hatching

Use an inverted spoon-point nib to create this subtle inverted vertical brick pattern, which is useful for backgrounds.

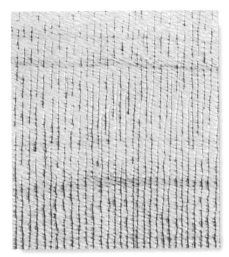

Graduated hatchings

Use an inverted spoon-point nib and put in parallel hatchings. Start each line slowly and speed up gradually, allowing less time for burning so the line fades gradually.

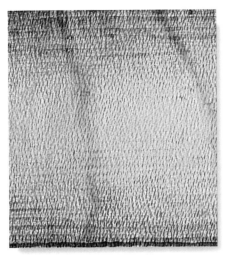

Painterly fade

Use the spoon-point nib to create a dark line by drawing the bowl horizontally across the bottom of the square, slowly. Continue to put in horizontal lines until you reach the centre, working each successive line a little faster to produce a fade. Repeat from the top downwards. Note: this is quite difficult to achieve.

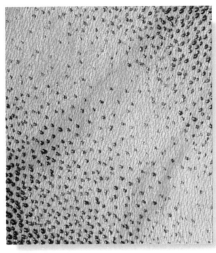

Dot fade

Use the standard nib to put in dots closely where you want a darker effect and more sparsely when you want a lighter effect. This technique is good for giving the impression of foliage.

Cross-hatch fade

Use an inverted spoon-point to build up layers of directional hatchings as with the dot fade.

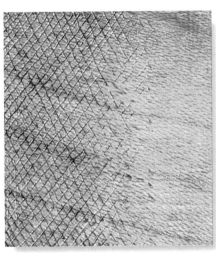

Mixed fade

This is a layered shading. First, use the bowl of a spoon-point nib to create a painterly fade from left to right. Then use the inverted spoon-point to accentuate the fade with a cross-hatched shading.

Light painterly effect

The inverted spoon-point nib is used on a low heat to create a slight overall tone to your wood. This may be used as a background 'wash' to line work.

Borders

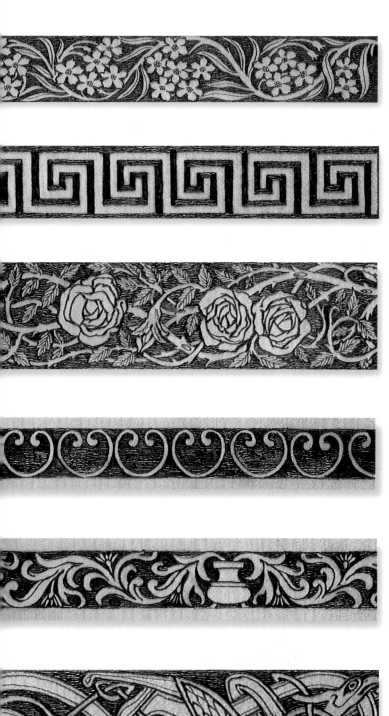

Borders are a popular device for the pyrographer, not least because they can be executed relatively easily, and on most surfaces. They can be used to frame a pyrography picture, or simply stand alone as ornamentation to an interesting piece of wood. For these reasons, borders will feature prominently throughout this book.

Victorian poker-work was predominantly made up of borders. This reflects both the decorative nature and the ease of construction of these designs. The primitive tools available a century ago were not capable of the intricacies of modern pyrography machines, but could be used successfully to outline, and block in behind, a feature such as a flowing vine. With modern tools there are fewer constraints on the choice of complicated border designs, but the technique of building them up remains the same.

A selection of borders is shown left, covering a range of different approaches: flowing foliate borders, geometric repeated patterns and Celtic designs can all be used, depending on the subject matter. Some borders are more formal and are contained units, fixed within the parameters of the border, whilst others appear to spill out beyond the edges. Old book illustrations offer a multitude of further designs, usually in pen-and-ink work, which are easy to adapt to the medium of pyrography.

When planning borders, only the strictly geometric examples need be measured out to ensure that repeated patterns are of uniform size. In general, borders will need to be sketched freehand. The panel opposite shows how corners may be tackled and includes motifs you may find useful. Most patterns can be adapted to go around corners, but if in doubt, you can simply fit a square device, such as a stylised flower, into each corner. This allows you to treat each of the four sides as a separate entity.

Borders

Planning the corners is the most complicated aspect of creating borders, but the design ideas opposite should help. Another way of dealing with corners is simply to insert a box like the examples shown.

Chessboard border

Once your chessboard squares are completed, you will be ready to add the border, which gives a decorative dimension to your sampler. My border (see below) was derived from natural sources, working up a pattern from sketches of a blackthorn bush. With its white blossoms, it is evocative of oriental art and ties in nicely with the Chinese origins of chess.

Constructing the border

You will see that a narrow inner border of plain wood has been left between the chessboard and the worked outer border. This is so that the outer border does not appear to bleed into any of the worked chessboard squares, especially any that are similarly worked. This internal border should be so thin as to be barely perceptible, and of a regular width.

When creating this border design, I included the flowers and the fruit of the plant to add interest. Draw these elements first as the branches can be interwoven to connect them. Leaves and thorns may be positioned wherever you like, and in this way, the design may be balanced, with no areas more or less busy than others.

When you begin to burn your design, build up the outlines first using a standard nib, then block in the background. This will provide the necessary information on your chosen wood's potential to burn in a controlled manner, and will allow you to decide whether or not to add further detail. I have added veining to the leaves, detail to the flowers, and shading to give the illusion of depth to the berries and branches.

Chessboard border

You may wish to copy this border, or you could follow a similar procedure, using your own sketches to build up a suitable design. Another alternative is to use one of the designs shown on pages 30 and 31.

Circular borders

Pyrography is a slow medium, but a time-efficient way to produce lovely pieces is to decorate only part of them. Circular borders can be designed to fit any turned piece, but are especially suited to rimmed bowls like the ones shown here. They remain functional objects, and can be used without obscuring the decoration.

It is a joy to work on finely crafted objects, and I usually use circular borders when I work on bowls made by local wood-turners. Pieces should have a rim at least 25mm (1in) wide to allow room to work, but this is still not a lot of surface area to fill. Distinctive woods and pyrography are not ideal partners, but dark border designs can be burned into almost any wood. They offer the opportunity to explore different types.

When you choose a border design, consider floral patterns as the flowing curves will mimic the arcs of the bowl. Geometric modern designs with straight lines and acute angles can also work surprisingly well. I am influenced by the Arts and Crafts Movement, which began in England in about 1875. Inspired by William Morris, Edward Burne-Jones and Dante Gabriel Rossetti, it heralded a return to traditional decorative techniques. The Kelmscott Press, which is a particular influence, produced highly-decorated books harking back to medieval manuscripts. Borders overflow with great sweeps of leaves, fruit and flowers, elements of which can be taken and made to follow the curve of a bowl. You could also learn from the lessons of the chessboard border, adopting the rules and formulas used by the artists mentioned above, but choosing your own natural forms to create a border.

Opposite
Decorated bowl

This design on a lacewood bowl was adapted from the border of an illustration by Aubrey Beardsley. After sketching out the design there were some spaces which I broke up by leaving small circles of unworked wood. These circles echoed the similar circles which were part of the original design, so the additions are in keeping. The result is a balanced design.

Opposite, below
Smaller bowls

An alternative way of working with smaller bowls is to use what are essentially borders to create a central design. The first of these, on apple wood, uses images originally found on a Japanese plate; the second, on silver birch, draws heavily on Celtic knotwork techniques, and the third, on sycamore, is a 20th-century floral design.

Simple rim decoration

A rimmed bowl needs no further decoration than this example in brown oak.

Project
Cheeseboard

This design works well on circular boards, rimmed platters, or indeed any turned pieces. The project uses a sycamore bread board, and shows how easily floral subjects can be adapted to produce borders. Sand the board well to prepare the surface before you begin.

Allow for a border about 25mm (1in) in diameter, beginning its outer edge a few millimetres in from the edge of the wood. When you are sketching borders, always draw the predominant motif – in this case the daisies – first. These should be spaced evenly, though they do not need to be planned with mathematical precision. To maintain the natural air of the subject, no one area should be significantly busier than another. It is important to strike a balance between natural chaos and aesthetic order.

Once your flowers are placed, they can be joined with stems to imitate the threaded nature of a daisy chain. Stems should again be random, flowing and drawn lightly so leaves and ancillary flower buds can be added later if an area seems to require filling. The balance between the areas of dark and light in the design should be roughly equal.

When you have sketched your design, follow the same steps using the pyrography tool. Outline the flowers, stems and leaves, and darken the background. When this is complete, you may wish to add further detail, picking out individual petals. I have built up each daisy centre with tiny circles. Leaves can be veined and shadows added to where one stalk passes over another. When you are working with dark and light borders, do not be tempted to add too much detail, or your design may not be distinct from the blocked-in background.

You will need

Circular sycamore board

Pencil

Pyrography tool fitted with standard point

A pair of compasses

Eraser

These sketches show how a straight design may be adapted to go round a curve.

Use compasses to draw in the circles to contain your border, spacing these about 25mm (1in) apart. Sketch your design so it is just bold enough to see. If you make a mistake, you can simply erase it and draw in the correct design.

Cheeseboard

Pyrography is amazingly resilient on cutting surfaces, so do not be afraid to use an item just because it has a picture on it.

Decorated plate

This plate was decorated using a design taken from an antique plate design for the border, and a different design as the inset. This demonstrates how border compositions leave you the opportunity of adding further decoration of your choice.

Building up tones

This exercise expands on the idea of creating lines of differing tones – see the note on page 17. Butterflies are a popular subject, and an excellent way to practise using cross-hatchings to build tone. A pyrography tool is the perfect vehicle for achieving the subtleties of shading represented in their wings. Some areas of the wings are clearly delineated, creating crisp edges; elsewhere, colours fade from dark to light through a range of mid-tones. Some of the shadings used to create the chessboard can be used to describe different areas of the butterfly.

Shading exercise

The butterflies shown right are built up entirely from shading: no outline is needed to describe the edge of the wing. You will need a good detailed pencil sketch of each butterfly to begin. If you usually draw freehand, you may wish to cheat a little: as we all know, butterfly wings are symmetrical. Draw one side freehand and trace it, then simply flip the tracing paper to complete the other side.

The example shows how the shapes of different butterflies can be built up by layering very fine lines in different directions. To create these fine lines, I invert the spoon-point nib of my pyrography tool and use the very fine edge. Note that even the preliminary hatchings over the wings and body are of differing intensities and are already starting to build up the light and dark tones. The direction of these first-stage marks is also deliberate, with the wings radiating from the body and curved shadings on the body to suggest depth.

In the next stage, cross-hatchings are added. This is similar to the technique used by cartoonists but more versatile: to vary the tones of your cross-hatching you can speed up, slow down or increase pressure (see above). Finally, more hatchings are added to the cross-hatched area, then blocks of hatching in mid-tones are added to the background, leaving some areas untouched to accentuate your work.

Note

When you illustrate a three-dimensional object, the shadings you put in should not be flat, but should echo the contours of the subject matter.

Sycamore platter

Butterflies have been used randomly to decorate this platter. Use them in the same way to decorate any surface you choose.

Butterfly progressions

This sycamore plaque shows stages in the completion of three kinds of butterfly. The shadings used are similar to the cross-hatching techniques used in the chessboard chapter, but each line of hatching is curved to mirror the contours of the subject.

Project
Milking stool

This project is fairly challenging because of its intricacy and the relatively large surface area covered. A three-legged milking stool is an ideal base for more advanced designs because the top is flat and easily worked, and the legs can be glued in place when the piece is finished. This design could take up to two days to complete, but you could work to a simplified design incorporating some of the same techniques.

Nursery rhymes are a good source of ideas because the information needed to construct the design is all contained within the rhyme. If you have a favourite drawing it is fairly simple to adapt it to fit a circular format. If you adapt someone else's work and plan to sell it, make sure you understand the laws of copyright. The design for this project is my own, but I looked at the ways in which other illustrators had tackled the same theme before. Wherever possible, I have introduced variation to the design to add interest. The patterns shown on pages 24-29 should provide inspiration.

Sketch

My own sketch for the stool top is very detailed, but the design could be simplified.

1.   Sand the stool to prepare the surface. Using a sharp pencil draw a border just inside the edge of your stool top to form the outer boundary of your design: you can use a plate as a guide. Though it looks good if you fill as much of the surface of the stool as possible, it is not easy to work up the edge without it looking untidy. Next, sketch the design lightly inside the border. Try to include all the outlines, but some of the detail can be left until later.

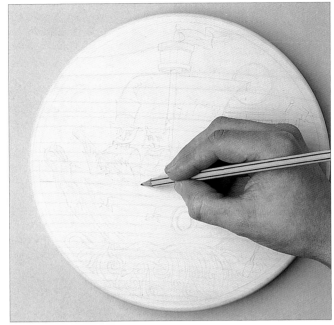

2.   When I work to such an ambitious design, I divide the picture into areas of similar shadings and treat each area as a separate picture. This piece takes some time to work, so the separate sections make it easier to pick up and put down again over a period of days or even weeks. Note that there are no discernible outlines; even though this is not a naturalistic subject, avoiding them will give the finished picture greater depth.

   Begin with the stylised waves, building them up with curved shadings following the direction of each foam tendril. Add hatching at 90° to your work to create shadow under each tendril. For the fish, use shading that imitates scales. Add a curved highlight to make the bottle shine.

3.   Build up the detail on the boat using a wood-grain effect on the timbers (see page 27). Take care to shade each plank separately; the grain should not run from one plank to the next. The nameplate on the boat has been left unworked but can be personalised. Shade the portholes to suggest bulls' eye glass and create the illusion of depth. Introduce shadows with cross-hatchings. Further layers of shading can be added at the end when you have an overall picture of any areas that look under-worked.

4. Add the remainder of the woodwork so the boat begins to look realistic. To mimic the effect of light reflections on glass, do not darken the windows completely. Note that the area under the sail is the darkest part of the picture and is a good measure for your other tones. It is built up with cross-hatchings, not just solid tone. If you use similar shading techniques throughout a piece it gives it a unity of design.

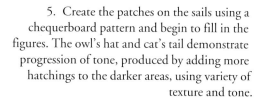

5. Create the patches on the sails using a chequerboard pattern and begin to fill in the figures. The owl's hat and cat's tail demonstrate progression of tone, produced by adding more hatchings to the darker areas, using variety of texture and tone.

6. Complete the figures of the owl and the pussycat. These are the central, most important part of the picture, so they have been given more detailed treatment. This can be extremely effective in pyrography, and has parallels with painting, in that greater realism is often used for the human elements in a picture, especially faces, while backgrounds and inanimate things are left deliberately sketchy.

The finished picture

The boat and the foreground were completed using more detail than the sea behind, then the sky using less detail than for the sea. This camera-lens focus also helps with perspective. Finally, the stool top was finished using the oil technique shown on pages 50-51.

Dragon stool

This sycamore stool is one of my original designs. The pyrography was built up with a mixture of painterly effects using a spoon-point nib and hatchings using a standard nib.

Decorated stools

Stools provide an enticing canvas for all kinds of designs. The large, flat working area allows for maximum detail and ceramic designs offer a virtually limitless source of inspiration for the pyrographer. Animals make ideal subjects for nursery stools, and the peacock stool was adapted loosely from an Arts and Crafts design. The other stool is based on a traditional Celtic knotwork design.

Project
Napkin rings

These napkin rings are made using faux marquetry. This technique demonstrates the painterly effects that can be achieved with your pyrography tool, as well as the potential for creating the illusion of depth. Emery paper is used to create reverse pyrography, lightening the wooden area to give your work a lift.

The napkin rings I used were made to order by a local wood-turner. The inner, worked ring of maple wood is set off by outer rings of darker African hardwood. It is not essential to use napkin rings for this technique: I have also used these geometric designs as banding around items including boxes and mirrors. Furniture makers over the centuries have used marquetry and parquetry in much the same way to embellish their work. Books on antique furniture are a good source for your designs.

If you use a rounded nib on your pyrography pen, in this case the bowl of a spoon-point, designs can be built up with blocks of colour rather than lines, dots or other mark-making techniques. Pyrography usually has more in common with pen-and-ink techniques, but this method is more like wash painting. The difficulty with this technique is producing uniform tones and eradicating any evidence of stroke marks. It is relatively easy to produce a uniform dark colour with pyrography because wood will only burn so much. To create areas of consistent mid-tone, you must work on a low heat, very slowly. Do not remove the nib between starting and finishing an area; avoid blotching by keeping it moving.

Sketch your design lightly on your work with pencil before you begin. This is fairly challenging and can really only be done by eye, since measuring on something so small is very fiddly. It may take a few attempts, but do not be put off; it becomes easier with practice.

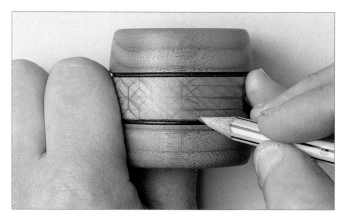

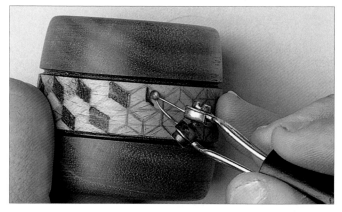

1. Pencil three equidistant horizontal lines round the central section of the napkin ring to divide the working area into four equal strips. Using the centre line as a guide, draw in a flattened diamond shape. Repeat this all the way round. Where two diamonds meet, draw a vertical line from the top horizontal to the bottom horizontal. Draw a vertical line to the edge from the upper and lower points of each diamond, draw a vertical to the edge. Join these lines with diagonals.

2. From now on, you should disregard the horizontal pencil lines so remove them if you wish, taking care not to erase your box pattern. Fill in one side of each box, making it as dark as possible, taking care not to go over your pencil lines.

The template below shows how the sections of the napkin ring are built up.

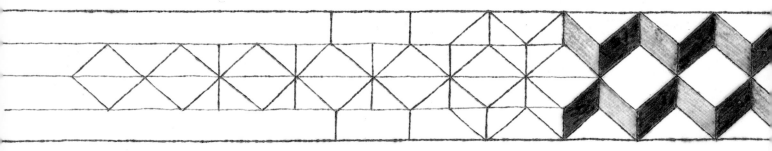

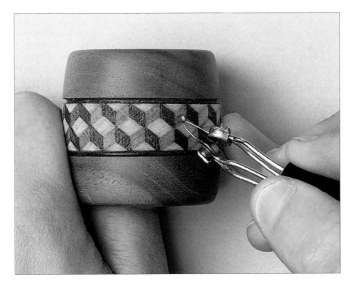

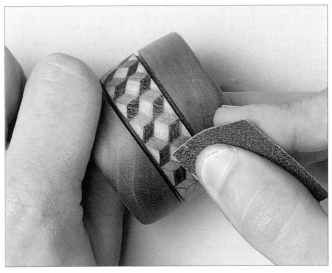

3. Turn down the heat on your machine and block in the opposite side of each box carefully in a uniform mid-tone. Note that the box edges are not defined with outlines but are suggested with different coloured planes to give the appearance of marquetry.

4. Fold a small square of emery paper in half to produce a stiff edge. Using the corner of this fold, scrape at the areas of bare wood to lighten them and enliven the tonal contrasts. As the emery paper becomes ineffective, fold it in another place and begin again. In this way, a small piece will last a long time.

A selection of napkin rings completed using faux marquetry techniques

Working with spheres

I have long admired the peculiar apple- or pear-shaped Georgian tea caddies that can be seen in the windows of high-class antique shops. Hand-turned in fruit woods and ornately finished with silver locks, they are now highly sought after and very expensive. I decided I wanted to work on something similar. I knew that the best wood-turners can produce almost anything, and I managed to find one based in the north of England. He now makes me batches of very high quality boxes in my choice of wood, lime.

The advantage of using truly high quality materials is that you can afford to invest real time and effort in them. I treat them like Japanese *netsuke* ware and cover every available surface, even those that are not normally seen.

Working on curved surfaces presents fresh – but not insurmountable – challenges for the pyrographer. Curved surfaces on a basic level – the tree vase and the faux marquetry napkin rings – have already been tackled, but attempting to work a highly elaborate design on a curved surface is a more advanced skill. Nevertheless, it is worth pursuing, not least because it offers far greater freedom for your choice of wood blank.

There are no short cuts when designing pictures for curved surfaces. It is no use trying to transfer designs with tracing or carbon paper, but you can adapt preliminary sketches to provide a guide. I often work from long, straight pictures that can be curled around the shape during the sketching-on process. No amount of preparatory sketching, however, can account for the distorting effects of the curved surface, most of your planning must be done on the wood. Try sketching and re-sketching lightly in pencil until you are happy with the image.

The wood I have used here is lime, which has a barely perceptible grain. These boxes allow for the very finest detail possible using pyrography. I have used an inverted spoon-point nib and short, minute hatchings to work all the examples shown. The short strokes mean that I do not have to work round much of a curve at any time.

Butterfly apple

These butterflies were worked in the same way as those in the exercise on pages 38 and 39. The lime wood used for these apples is of a better quality for burning, so the example shows a wider range of tones. When working on a curved surface, I sometimes allow the design to develop of its own accord rather than planning the layout in advance. In this case, each butterfly was placed randomly and worked before the next was sketched on. I knew that with such a huge variety of butterflies to choose from, plus the option of making up my own, I could just work around the apple and fill any gaps later. I removed the stalk of the apple for ease of working, and used emery paper at the end of the process to give a greater tonal range to the design.

House apple

This is another design adaptation, this time from the whimsical houses theme on pages 52 – 57. In this example, it is easy to see the distorting effect of curved surfaces. The flat design was sketched round the apple, but as the girth of the apple varies considerably from top to bottom, so too does the design. In this case, it makes the houses look top-heavy. With a subject such as medieval houses this does not matter as the jettied construction of the buildings justifies the distortion. In other cases, allowances can be made during the sketching process. I think it is inadvisable to choose naturalistic designs for such a shaped surface, so I tend to opt for whimsical subjects as they still look good when distorted.

Finishing your work

There is some debate about whether or not to add a finish to pyrography. Work should certainly be left bare if further pyrography, such as personalised lettering, is to be added to a design. In some cases, customers may wish to choose their own finish for a piece, or they may just prefer wood to be left in its natural state. It is an unfortunate fact that wood-burning, just like watercolour painting, will fade if exposed to light. Over time, base woods will also deepen in colour so the pyrography will appear to fade. A wood finish will go some way towards protecting work against the effects of light and age. Though tastes and fashions vary, here are some handy hints which may inform your choices regarding the finish on your work:

Danish oil and a soft rag

• The biggest drawback is that most finishes must be applied to a perfectly smooth and sanded surface, but sanding a surface that is wood-burnt may remove some of your work.

• The effect of any reverse pyrography on your work may be compromised by the application of a finish. This will depend on the finish and the wood, so experiment on a hidden area first.

• Varnish, once popular with pyrographers, may obscure fine detail. As a general rule, I use varnish only on pieces that are to be displayed outdoors, such as house signs. In this case, use yacht varnish. A clear matt varnish may be appropriate for items such as pencil boxes that are likely to be handled a lot.

• Wax may be suitable, though furniture waxes can appear streaky when applied. The finish should be as unobtrusive as possible, so it is best to avoid coloured finishes that may detract from your work. Even lighter coloured woods are best left their natural colour.

• Danish oil is my preferred choice for all work. It brings out the grain of the wood and gives it a lift without streaking or appearing obtrusive. It is available from hardware stores and can be brushed or wiped on in one or more coats.

• For the best information about finishes, speak to wood-turners. They tend to be very knowledgeable on the subject. Remember that finishes designed to be applied on a lathe may not be so easy to apply evenly by hand.

1. Always use fine sand paper to remove any marks or discoloration on your wood. This especially applies to edges , which may discolour due to contact with the oils in your hands while you are working .

2. Apply Danish oil evenly with a rag or brush.

The finished plate

When dry, the Danish oil adds colour without concealing the detailed work. It may even serve to lift the picture by adding contrast. Further coats may be added according to preference.

DESIGN

I rarely repeat a picture exactly. This is to keep each piece individual, which is the main advantage a hand-craft has over industrial processes. In any case, repeat items seldom have the freshness of an original design, and your technique will not improve if you simply repeat pieces. Starting from scratch, however, is not always practical. If you produce a lot of pyrography work, for sale or pleasure, it is always helpful to have certain themed or formulaic ways of producing designs quickly. It is well worth exploring the idea of creating your own themes, which can become a personal trademark of your work.

Developing a theme

I consider myself lucky to live in the heart of Suffolk, a county particularly rich in historic architecture and therefore packed with inspiration. I sketch interesting and unusual houses that I see, or sometimes just details like chimneys, oriel windows and arched doorways. From these sketches, I can construct whole street scenes of places that have never really existed. If I am working to order, I can personalise these street scenes by adding a client's favourite pub or incorporating a specific house. I developed this particular way of working many years ago and it has proved inexhaustible.

Photographs are excellent to work from. Photographic developers offer a range of services, including black and white reproductions from colour negatives, and now even sepia reproductions, which are ideally suited to pyrography as they provide tonal references for shading. They are an invaluable source of reference for producing sketches, which in turn can be built up to fit exactly any shape of object you choose.

Source photograph

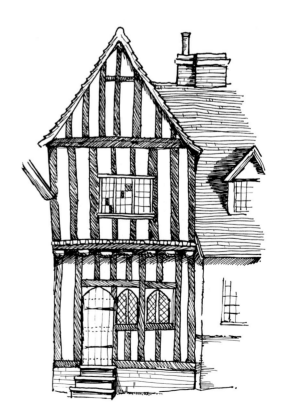

In my sketch I have straightened the appearance of the house so it will be easier to reproduce

Project
Whimsical house box

This project is a useful and interesting exploration of the links between cartooning and pyrography. I have somewhat exaggerated the medieval aspects of my chosen house – see photograph and initial sketch opposite – rather like cartooning.

I began by drawing a rectangle on paper to represent the available surface area and adapting my chosen house to suit the space. The actual house is sandwiched between others in a street, but I have adapted it into a detached house to give clear outlines around the edge, and extended its width to better fill the space. I have added decorative 'carving' to the main beams to provide an interesting contrast in texture, and given it a thatched roof instead of tiles. Experience has taught me that thatch is easier to represent in pyrography than roof tiles!

The most common approach to wood-burning is to describe features using line. Just as in pen-and-ink work, elements of a picture can be built up using different shadings, with shadows added as a final touch to give depth. The lime card-box I used is light in colour, close-grained and finely finished, which means there are no constraints on detail or tonal range.

You will need

Small lime box

Soft pencil

Eraser

Pyrography tool

Spoon-point nib

The simplified sketch I used as a template

1. With a pencil transfer the outlines of your design to the lid of the box. Use as few lines as possible and work lightly, so your pencil lines can be removed easily.

2. Follow the pencil lines using the inverted edge of a spoon nib. To make my work more realistic, I tend to avoid outlining, but the whimsical nature of this project means that outlines are acceptable. Work lightly on a low heat; some of the outlines will be darkened up at a later stage, others are more for guidance, indicating the perimeters of the different areas of shading.

3. Begin to shade in the details. The beams are shaded using a wood-grain texture (see page 27). Suggest brickwork by indicating the pattern roughly, rather than by drawing each individual brick, The thatch is built up with strokes graduated from dark at the top and fading to nothing. To do this, begin each stroke slowly and speed up. Darken the windows, leaving areas of white to suggest the division between different window panes.

The finished box

The final detail has been added by cross-hatching the thatch diagonally, from both left to right and right to left, in the same graduated strokes, to produce an overall progression of tone. I have placed the light source in the top right-hand corner and added cross-hatched shadows accordingly. The left-hand side of the beams have been darkened to make them stand out, and shadows placed where appropriate to add greater depth. I have also added fanciful details to give the design narrative and appeal: the inn sign, the rooftop washing line and the patterned main beams. Finally, a thick black outline makes the picture stand out from the background.

Sketches

If you select details randomly from sketch books, inventing extra details as you go along, your designs will always be different though they will look similar.

Pencil box

Some shaped objects can prove problematic when choosing designs. For long, thin objects like this pencil box a street scene always works well, as buildings can be added in a linear manner without affecting the composition.

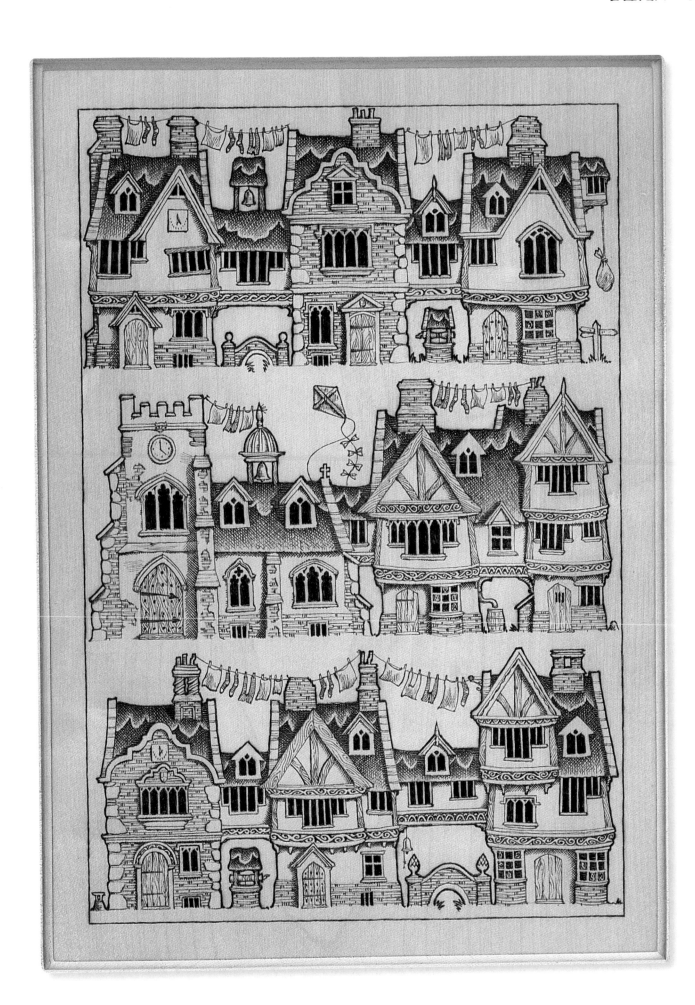

Fairies

Photography, especially of figures, was influential in the development of modern art. It meant that the fleeting moment could be captured better than ever before and scenes looked less posed. Pyrography struggles to attain a reputation for contemporary design, perhaps because the process is so slow, and cannot easily replicate the freedom of movement and line of other art and craft mediums. Working from photographs, and sketches produced from photographs, can add a modernity to the craft, and I often take my own to work from, as in the fairy platter shown on page 61. I use an old-fashioned dip pen for sketching, which creates an uneven width of line and often produces happy accidents. With careful use of your pyrography pen, this uneven line can be imitated.

The project came about at a time when flower fairies were in vogue and many customers were commissioning flower fairy christening gifts. I began by adapting designs from the classic Cicely Mary Barker illustrations, but much as I admired the original pictures, they were designed for children and can look rather 'chocolate boxy'. I wanted designs that were modern and more grown-up. Under duress, a friend agreed to be a fairy for the day. She was suitably attired in fairy wings and bedecked with flowers, and we trekked to a local wood for photographs. These photographs were revisited many times as source material for a series of pen and ink sketches, some of which are shown here. I decided which sketches worked best, then developed them into my final design.

The next step was to buy a gigantic platter from a wood-turner's stand at a craft fair. It is about 75cm (2ft 6in) in diameter, made from solid walnut, and not surprisingly was expensive. Starting on such a piece can be a nerve-racking proposition, but fortunately, this project could be broken down into smaller parts. Each figure was tackled as an individual project, and the background linking all these elements was added afterwards to unify the whole. There were knots in the surface of the wood, but as I planned each element I simply avoided them. The polished surface caused more problems and for this reason, despite appearances to the contrary, detail and work was kept to a minimum. It took the equivalent of two weeks' work to complete the whole project.

Black and white photographs can act as a tonal template for pyrography work

These quick sketches made from photographs helped to inform the style of pyrography in the final piece

Fairy platter

For this platter, I allowed myself the liberty of using outlines to define the figures, which I felt was necessary on such dark wood. I kept the outlines as fine as possible so that they did not detract from the picture when they were combined with the dense background shading.

Details

The design was built up with a range of shading techniques: dots to express the uneven and busy woodland floor; curved cross-hatchings to give depth to the trees, and delicate hatchings to describe the figures. Finally, the background was punctuated by areas of soft shading amongst the trees to show the dappled play of light you see in dense woodland.

Birds

Certain themes seem to lend themselves to pyrography, and I find myself returning again and again to birds. If you are producing for potential profit as well as for pleasure, certain subjects are clearly more saleable than others. Birds are almost universally popular, especially owls, birds of prey and exotic varieties such as peacocks. This section shows how pyrography is particularly suited to describing the texture of feathers and the play of light and shade distinctive to birds' plumage.

One advantage of choosing birds as subjects is the vast breadth of illustrative books on the subject. These are often illustrated with colour or black and white photos, watercolours and pen & ink sketches, all of which can be useful when developing designs. Bird books illustrated with wood engravings are particularly helpful: woodcut illustrations make excellent templates. Birds are popular with engravers for the same reasons as for pyrographers: the mark-making techniques of each medium mimic the visual texture of the birds. Though wood-engraving works in negative – the marks made appear as white on a print – the skills used in wood-engraving transfer readily to pyrography.

The art of pyrography is not always used in isolation: craftsmen working in many different fields use it to complement their work. This includes wood-turners, who use it to sign and document their work; marqueteurs, who use it to introduce tonal variation to their veneers, and makers of decoy ducks, who use it once the carving process is completed. In this case, the pyrography tool is used as a carving implement, to gouge the wood and give it the texture of feathers before painting it. When the colours of the duck are added, the feathering can still be seen. In pyrography, there is no need to gouge at the wood when replicating the feathers of birds, but the pattern of feathers can be imitated in a similar way to record the image.

Golden plover

This picture on a sycamore plaque is well balanced within the available space, but still leaves enough room to add a house name or number. It was inspired by a Charles Tunnicliffe woodcut. Woodcuts cleverly use not only dark outlines and shading but also white. Different areas can be defined in a naturalistic way by leaving the faintest outlines of un-burnt wood in areas of densely burnt wood, producing the appearance of lines of white shading on a black area. Using this technique, the best wood-engravers appear to work not only in dark and light but also in light on dark. With care, this negative technique is possible in pyrography and you might like to try it.

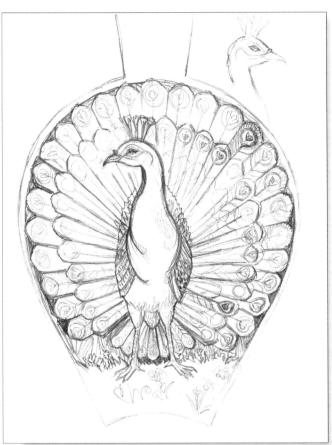

Peacock bellows

The large expanse of flat surface on bellows makes them an ideal canvas for pyrography. Craftspeople are often prepared to barter skills, and I obtained these bellows when I decorated another set for a local maker. In exchange, he made me a set in sycamore to my specifications.

The traditional 'ace of spades' shape of bellows immediately suggested a peacock design, which fits the space exactly. My inspiration came not from bird studies in ornithological books, but rather from the stylised representations seen in the Arts and Crafts movement's ceramics and textiles. I was particularly inspired by William Morris, but the final creation is my own.

Though stylised, the image is shaded using a similar approach to the naturalistic golden plover opposite. The fanned tail is built up with flowing hatchings, following the form of each feather; the body with feathered strokes, again following the contours of the bird. The dark background pushes the bird forward, and the eye was worked carefully so that it would seems to look directly at the observer. As a functional object, the bellows were finished with several coats of Danish oil.

Template

A line template (below) is useful for planning out designs and transferring them on to wood.

Tawny owl

This imposing owl was adapted from a woodcut by Charles Tunnicliffe, who is possibly the greatest bird artist, and worked on a sycamore breadboard . One objective pyrographers may work towards is producing work that uses as broad a range of tones as possible. Bird pictures like this are a useful exercise because they exploit a kind of 'sepia rainbow' of tones. Very dark and very light tones are easy to achieve, but the range of mid-tones is more difficult. The greater the range of these tones you can introduce to your work, the more potential you have for depicting form. Note that the shadings on this bird mimic the contours of the body and the lines on each feather fan out from each quill. The tree trunk and foliage imitate some of the mark-making signature of wood-engraving.

Swan pencil block

This shows the decorated side panel of a small sycamore pencil block, used as a desk tidy for pencils and pens. The swan is taken from a Norman Thelwell pen-and-ink study, and the lines that build up the picture imitate Thelwell's cross-hatching. Even on a small scale, hatchings – though not describing every feather of a bird – can still suggest the texture of the subject.

Pyrography has an advantage over pen and ink because it offers a greater tonal range. A white swan must be tackled in a sensitive fashion as the shadows and tonal changes suggesting the different areas on the bird are very slight. Using shadows that are very light in tone, pyrography makes this swan look three-dimensional, while retaining the illusion of a white bird.

Barn owl board

This design on a sycamore chopping board was again inspired by a Tunnicliffe woodcut. Although the colour range in pyrography is limited to varying hues of browns, sometimes a picture may echo the range of colour seen in nature – as is the case with this owl. Wherever possible, I like to fill the pieces of wood I use, but when working in such fine detail, a smaller composition can save a lot of time and effort. This picture is a compromise as it is large enough to command attention; filling the whole board might have taken twice as long without producing any discernible increase in impact.

This example demonstrates how, seen from a distance, the individual cross-hatchings merge into overall areas of varying tone. I used an inverted spoon-point nib throughout.

Animals

The examples here show how effective animals can be in pyrography. They also show how the methods used to design on spheres can be adapted for working inside bowls.

The theme of animals suits pyrography for the same reasons as for birds. The shadings serve a dual purpose: they build up tone while also imitating the appearance of an animal's coat. The chessboard project which begins on page 25 shows how different shadings can be applied in various combinations to create an image. When working a naturalistic subject such as an animal, the hatching put in to represent shading should not be flat, but should follow the contours of the subject. The hair on a dog's coat, for example, follows the shape of the body, so the shadings used to recreate this must follow the direction of the hair to give depth and life to the resulting picture.

With practice, it becomes clear that some animal subjects are easier to reproduce than others. This may be because of the particular shape or texture of the animal: for example, I think hedgehogs are difficult. Or it could be because of the tonal range, which can be limited: I would rather draw a tabby cat than a completely black cat.

Wood-turners offer a great range of bowls, and one of these can make a beautiful starting point. Animal subjects can be sketched on the flat and literally curled to make perfect subjects for working on a curved surface. Take care when selecting a bowl to work on as not all will be suitable: with a small bowl that has steeply curved sides there may not be enough room to get your hand and pyrography tool comfortably inside. Ideally, you should look for relatively shallow bowls that slope gradually. These should be smoothed well, with interesting grains that are not too intrusive.

When burning on a curve, each stroke you make with your hand should rise or fall with the curve. Remember that in order to achieve even burning the nib should only *touch* the surface. The problem of burning on a gradient can be eased by choosing an animal subject that can be built up using small staccato strokes.

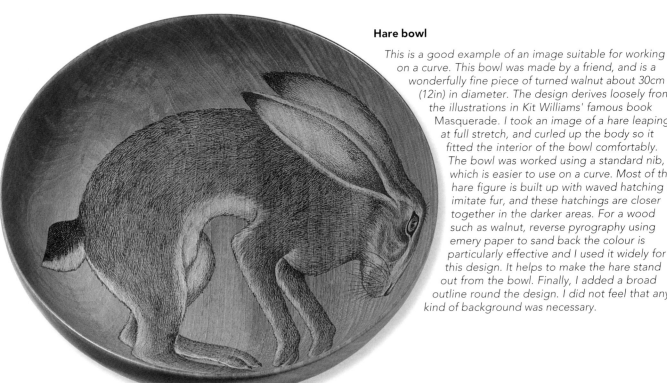

Hare bowl

This is a good example of an image suitable for working on a curve. This bowl was made by a friend, and is a wonderfully fine piece of turned walnut about 30cm (12in) in diameter. The design derives loosely from the illustrations in Kit Williams' famous book Masquerade. I took an image of a hare leaping at full stretch, and curled up the body so it fitted the interior of the bowl comfortably. The bowl was worked using a standard nib, which is easier to use on a curve. Most of the hare figure is built up with waved hatching to imitate fur, and these hatchings are closer together in the darker areas. For a wood such as walnut, reverse pyrography using emery paper to sand back the colour is particularly effective and I used it widely for this design. It helps to make the hare stand out from the bowl. Finally, I added a broad outline round the design. I did not feel that any kind of background was necessary.

Chase scene bowl

The circular area inside bowls offers great scope for design. Most of the curvature of the bowl is in the steeply-stepped sides, so I concentrated only on the slightly curved centre. This walnut bowl is quite large: 36cm (14in) in diameter. Its steep edges made working inside it quite difficult, so I had to hold the pen at a more acute angle than was comfortable. This design is really an extension of the idea of the concentric circle that informs the hare bowl opposite. I worked from life sketches, but gave the animals a slightly comical look. The sketches (below) show how flat designs can be curved and adapted to fit the space neatly. When transferring these to the wood, designing becomes an organic process: as each element is added, so the next picture is adjusted to fit the space available. I used a standard point in my pyrography pen, working with small strokes to build up the design through texture. Heavy use of emery paper completed the design.

My sketches for the bowl

Architecture & the landscape

Buildings and the surrounding landscape make excellent subjects for a naturalistic approach. If you choose to work in this way, you will need all the different mark-making techniques in your arsenal to differentiate between the different planes and textures.

Landscape is undoubtedly the most common theme embraced by artists, not least because of the taste of the art-buying public; if you hope to sell your work, it is a lucrative subject. Many pyrographers earn good money producing commissions of people's houses, and pictures of churches are very popular to commemorate weddings or anniversaries. The source material for designs is almost limitless. Old photographs of everyday life, in black and white or sepia, are particularly useful to work from. They can be beautifully crisp and detailed, with a broad tonal range. I usually work from architectural studies or rural scenes, making my own sketches or pen-and-ink washes. These provide a good tonal guide and make the resulting wood-burnings look loose and fresh.

Primarily, you will be attempting to capture the play of light and shadows, which will give your subject a naturalistic look. The range of tone and texture that can be seen in outdoor subjects makes building and landscapes one of the most difficult themes in pyrography but also, when done well, the most accomplished. Be prepared to cheat a little when designing – or, to put it more politely, use artistic licence. I always remove unattractive elements like pylons or guttering. Trees can be added to balance pictures both tonally and compositionally.

Church with round tower

Though naturalistic, this picture on a sycamore cheeseboard is more free than most of my architecture and landscape subjects. It took about three hours to pyrograph. A more impressionistic image can be produced if you work from a sketch rather than working painstakingly from a photograph: be bold and you will produce an attractive image much faster. I added detail and lifted tones with hatching, using a standard nib to build up blocks of shading on a low heat, copying the tones of the sketch. The varying thicknesses of the pen-and-ink lines were replicated by blocking in at a temperature higher than usual. Painters can use colour perspective to indicate distance, but pyrographers must attempt a regression of detail. Broadly speaking, the further away things are, the less focused and hazier they seem. This can be represented by loose, abstract hatchings. Do not be tempted to give objects in the background the same treatment as those in the foreground.

Extra time spent on a detailed template pays off when you burn your piece of wood: the process is faster, easier and produces better results. My initial sketch was taken from a black and white photograph. It was painted very freely, using different dilutions of black ink, and I tried to build it up in as broad a range of tones as possible. Pen-and-ink line drawing using a dip pen gave an uneven, naturalistic line to the painting.

Restored House, Boxford

Half-timbered buildings are excellent subjects for pyrography because it suits the combination of dark beams against light wood. This picture on a 225 x 170cm (9 x 7in) sycamore plaque was adapted from a pencil sketch by Suffolk artist Leonard Squirrell, who is one of my favourites. The choice of subject is always important: here the tremendously skilled draughtsmanship in the original shines through. Note the composition of the sky: this must never be allowed to blend into other elements of the picture and must appear to recede. To achieve this, I reserve specific hatchings to suggest clouds and depth.

This is my own drawing, but remember that the sketches you use to work from need not be so detailed – in fact, trying to work from complicated sketches may result in a less lively finished piece.

Hengrave Church

In contrast with the image opposite, a photo-realistic approach has been used for this picture on a 225 x 170cm (9 x 7in) sycamore plaque. I worked from a colour photograph so the pencil sketch took some time to produce. A significant problem of working from photographs is that the camera lens can sometimes distort angles. This may not be obvious when you look at a photograph, but if you try to trace the main features, or even copy them on a piece of wood using a carefully measured grid, your final image can look very wrong.

Planning can sometimes take many attempts. For this reason I always sketch very lightly, so that unwanted lines can be removed easily. When I tackle such a detailed subject, I like to sketch thoroughly, even down to individual bricks in the walls. In this way I can be sure that all the individual elements sit well together before I start burning.

The picture was built up from minute cross-hatchings, using an inverted spoon-point nib. Medieval churches often have several periods of construction, so the fabric of the building may contain different materials and textures. This adds tremendous variety, making them an ideal subject for wood-burning.

Lavenham

This was inspired by an Edwardian photograph and worked on a sycamore board 225 x 170cm (9 x 7in). The introduction of human elements to a landscape adds narrative to a picture. Technically, this was approached in a different way from the other examples on these pages. First, I added areas of tone using the bowl of a spoon-point nib, giving the picture a wash effect. I added the detail and shadings on top, using an inverted spoon-point nib. The area of water was particularly difficult to represent, but when you work from black and white photographs, you cannot go far wrong as long as you record the different tonal areas faithfully.

Laxfield Church Tower

Pyrography has a tendency to look traditional and old-fashioned, but you can give it a contemporary feel by using modernistic composition. One way to do this is to show the everyday from unexpected angles. The photograph that formed the starting point for this image was taken from an acute angle, which gave it gravitas. I tackled it in much the same way as the picture of Hengrave church on page 71, with a highly detailed pencil preparation. The different surfaces were built up with visual clues: for example, every time you see flint, the marks are made in the same way. Again, distance is suggested by a regression of tone and detail. I commission stepped frames for these plaques which, for a little extra cost, elevate them to artwork status.

Carving

Some years ago, my school art teacher suggested that I should diversify beyond pyrography. I set about carving a relief landscape on a lump of horse chestnut about 60cm (24in) long and 5cm (2in) thick. The scene shows a sweeping vista across the grounds of the Museum of East Anglian Life in Stowmarket, though I 'moved' the windmill closer to the water mill for composition purposes. I used very free sketches made on the spot and built up different planes of texture to indicate regression.

Horse chestnut is not an ideal wood for carving; I just used the first thing that came to hand. Consequently, the carving process was extremely long-winded, and I had grave difficulties throughout. The wood was very tough to chisel, and split and splintered off at unforeseen moments. The result, after two months of art classes, and despite vigorous sanding and smoothing, was pretty awful. It seemed fit for nothing.

In a final attempt to rescue my carving, I decided to wood-burn it. I used a coil nib for the uneven ploughed field in the foreground, and stippled most of the other areas with a standard point. Wood-burning mainly just accentuated the contours of the carving, but some of the details I added to the background gave the appearance of being carved because of the context. In this way, I was able to save a bad carving. Wood-burning appears to complement carving nicely, and to my knowledge this is a largely unexplored avenue of pyrography. If you are interested, however, be sure not to start with a piece of horse chestnut: the craftsman's choice is more likely to be lime or boxwood.

Opposite
Sketch

A pen-and-wash preliminary sketch. The angle of view in the finished piece has been influenced by the grain of the wood.

These are the photographs I used to help me plan the original carving

BRANCHING OUT

Most of the work featured so far was produced on pieces of wood designed and sold for pyrography. This type of wood is pale in colour, highly finished and without dramatic variations in grain. Working on a canvas of this kind, you can be fairly sure that it will allow very fine detail and a broad tonal range. Though it is undoubtedly the most *suitable* canvas for pyrography, this type of wood is bland and barely recognisable as wood. The finished piece, however accomplished, can lack the hues and figuring so beloved by wood enthusiasts. When I am displaying wood-burning at a craft fair or exhibition, I find it is better to have a variety of woods to excite the audience and antique pieces can give your plainer articles a lift.

Old and antique wood

There is great fun to be had searching for pieces to work on; I look in antique and junk shops, auctions and car-boot sales. In the past, wood was far more widely used, so there is plenty to choose from. It may also be inexpensive, though older and rarer items, often known as *treen,* are highly sought after. Remember that liking something does not guarantee success; many items I have bought have proved unsuitable after I have started work on them. I would advise you to buy cheaply and experiment so you learn to recognise the objects and woods that work best for you.

Detail of the finished cake stand

Opposite
A selection of old wooden pieces worked with pyrography.

Working on antique pieces

Before you start to work, you must discover as much as possible about your piece's limitations, so as to make informed choices regarding your design. Most importantly, you should establish how much detail and tonal contrast the wood will permit.

If the piece has a hidden surface, for example the bottom of a box, you could produce a miniature sampler or just a doodle. I often sign a piece before I start, and in this way I discover how the pyrography tool reacts with the wood. Note that some pieces may be made up of different woods: better woods may be reserved for the visible surfaces, or sometimes veneers may be used. If in doubt, start with a simple design, and add more detail if you find the wood is working well. Plan out your design and sketch it on using a very soft pencil (no harder than 2B), which will show up clearly even on very dark surfaces.

The beauty of working on old pieces is that they will often suggest subject matter to you. You may derive ideas from an object's previous function or its age. I try to add decoration that is sympathetic to a piece, and which could have been contemporary. With luck, it can appear as if a design newly-added to an old object has always been there. You can find ideas for designs from old furniture, textiles and ceramics.

You may have to work boldly to make your designs stand out. Emery paper is very useful: used effectively, it can work as a chalk to your charcoal, sanding back the years of coloration to give your work a third tone.

Victorian box

The marquetry effect on this mahogany box was created by sanding back areas with emery paper. Pyrography was used to add detail to the sanded areas.

The range of old wood is infinite and you will never find two identical pieces. You could look out for old wooden spoons, breadboards, turned bowls and other kitchenalia. With age and your decoration, these once-utilitarian objects can take on a new life as *objets d'art*. Old boxes – anything from pill or snuff-boxes and old pencil cases to writing slopes and smoking cabinets – work particularly well. The ambitious pyrographer could try decorating a stool, a chair or even a blanket box.

When working on old items, take care not to abuse a genuinely fine antique: a Victorian writing slope in perfect condition is a precious thing. It would not only be rash to attempt to improve on antique craftsmanship but it could prove to be an expensive mistake. But working sympathetically on a piece that has seen better days can restore some of its former appeal. With the current trend for shabby chic, or furnishings that look a bit distressed, buyers will gladly overlook the usual ravages of time such as missing pieces of veneer, dents or marks on the wood.

Identifying the woods used for old pieces can prove difficult. Time and years of polishing can change colour significantly. If you are lucky, you may come across a piece of rosewood, which burns beautifully. More likely, you will find mahogany, which was used profusely in the Victorian era, and can prove difficult to work on. Functional items like kitchenalia and old tools tended to be made from woods that are suitable for pyrography. They were not designed to look beautiful, but over the years, once-pale woods have taken on a richer colour, and decades of wear have smoothed such items, just ready for you to work on them.

Beware of pieces that have been stained a darker colour than the natural wood, a common device used to imitate more expensive woods. The staining will make working awkward and limit your designs. You should also avoid wood that is highly varnished and has a glossy finish, although more restrained finishes can be used to your advantage.

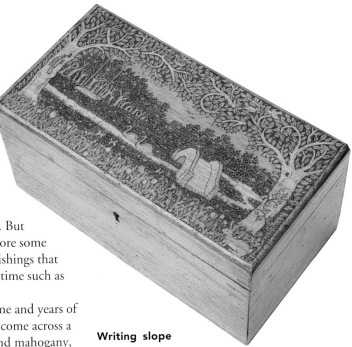

Writing slope

Boxes like these can be picked up relatively cheaply. The exterior was fine, but the interior had been lost. It is mahogany, so it did not burn very easily. I completed the initial design, a border of trees and grasses, before deciding to turn it into more of a landscape. The box was highly polished, so I used the pyrography tool on a high heat to draw the silhouetted trees in the background, and to add texture, simultaneously pushed the melted lacquer around .

Detail of writing slope

I used emery paper to create the lighter tones

Trompe l'oeil box

This Edwardian box was a great find in an antique shop. It was designed to look like a book, and the bottom of the 'spine' pulls out to reveal a hidden compartment made to contain a precious book. My design of a girl reading continues the book metaphor and is based on a Beardsley illustration. The trellis behind her echoes the fruit wood banding set into the box.

Opposite
Detail of box lid

Pencil box

Another small box, in this case a 1930s pencil box, was given a geometric design adapted from fabric of the period. When using very dark woods, it is best to stick to bold, clear designs.

Cabinet

This is an old smoker's cabinet, which I bought for its beautiful pewter doorknobs. The wood was really too dark to work on, so I used emery paper to remove the surface within the shape of the ladies and round the door edges. I was then able to work on the bare surfaces, mimicking Chinese lacquer work and marquetry.

Apple box

I used a silhouette of dancing animals wrapped round this box, as the dark wood would not permit anything more delicate by way of decoration.

Pine box

This box, which is about 30cm (12in) long, demonstrates the detail that can be achieved on a highly-smoothed pine surface. It is busily decorated with an outer border and inner silhouette. I used emery paper to strip back the years of coloration round the central silhouette, which is based on an Arthur Rackham design, to give the decoration an inlaid appearance.

Elephant money box

The painting I worked from

*I adapted this picture from cartoons in an old children's book.
The design was altered to fit the shape of the box.*

Dove

I added this dove to the original design to help balance the different elements.

Poodle

Changing the position of this circus dog helped to widen the picture.

The finished box

I picked up this old charity box, which might originally have sat on the bar in a public house, cheaply from a car boot sale. This one is plywood, but I have worked on several others and the wood used varies. I kept the design very sketchy, like my original painting, so accuracy of stroke was not important. I highlighted the figures against the background with emery paper and finished it with a liberal application of Danish oil, which made the design recede and gave the impression of age.

Finding wood

Unlike money, wood does grow on trees, and we are surrounded by suitable materials for pyrography. When you are starting out, you will probably need to look no further than the garden shed or garage for scraps of wood to practise on and build your confidence, with no fear of making expensive mistakes. Once you have jumped the initial hurdle of becoming comfortable with your machine, 'found' wood can both inspire you and help you to develop your art. Working with the unusual can give you ideas that carry over to the more everyday pieces.

Timber merchants and wood-turners may be a rich source of off-cuts of unworked wood for pyrography. These can be smoothed with a hand sander. Many of the best pyrographers let the grain of the wood work with their designs, inspiring or dictating the subject. An unfinished block of wood does not look very interesting: it should be sanded heavily to reveal the grain underneath. As the true surface emerges, your imagination can take over. The amount of work you do can be minimised by leaving areas blank and letting an interesting grain mimic, for example, a sunset or a brooding sky. Wood grains are a lottery, though certain woods are predictable: lacewood, for example, always appears to imitate the ripples of the sea.

Driftwood

If you have access to the coast or a river estuary, driftwood, which is bleached by the sea and contorted into strange forms, is a fantastic material for pyrography. Early 20th-century artists like Ben Nicholson recognised its aesthetic and often animal-like qualities, and it has been a popular medium for sculpture ever since. It will often lend itself to certain designs, and if you view a piece from different angles a likeness may suggest itself. Driftwood sculptors will surround themselves with collected pieces and wait for the gnarled features of one to inspire them, and this is the approach I prefer.

Driftwood is not all good news: most is unidentifiable. You may need to take pieces home and dry them out before you can decide whether they are suitable. One approach is to look for pieces which are smooth and do not have a very coarse grain. Be aware that burning, heavily-salted wood smells disgusting!

Despite the difficulties of working it, a few choice marks may be all that is needed to transform a piece of driftwood into something recognisable. Another option is to take a nautical approach: ships and seaside themes are eternally popular. Boats, seagulls and beach huts will combine with the grain of the wood to create seascapes. Where possible, work in silhouette: the wood may not allow anything else, and this looks particularly effective against the bleached wood.

Driftwood examples

These two pieces were found at Dunwich, in Suffolk, where a once great city was lost to the sea. Could these be relics from the submerged houses? The piece above, a heavy unidentified wood, I covered with knot-work, drawing from both Celtic and Maori influences. The piece below lent itself to this design, reminiscent of scrimshaw work. Old ship art has much in common with pyrography: sailors once etched on ivory and bone, and filled the scratches with soot. Referring to books on scrimshaw, you will find designs, which are very decorative, but crude enough to be imitated on the difficult surface of a piece of driftwood.

A magical discovery

I discovered this extraordinary block of wood (shown actual size), on a wood turner's stall at a craft fair. It is a piece of spalted beech, and – until I rescued it – it was about to be polished and mounted with a clock. Spaltering is caused by a fungal disease which invades dead wood and leaves these characteristic black lines. Once rejected by wood workers, it is now highly prized, and some turners have developed a technique of introducing spaltering artificially into newly-cut wood.

When I first saw it, the marking instantly suggested a coastline. The spalted area has formed an island and I simply took emery paper to the other areas to lighten what would become the sea. Taking inspiration from early seafaring maps, I illustrated all sides of the block.

The natural spaltering in the wood creates an impression of rocks and cliffs.

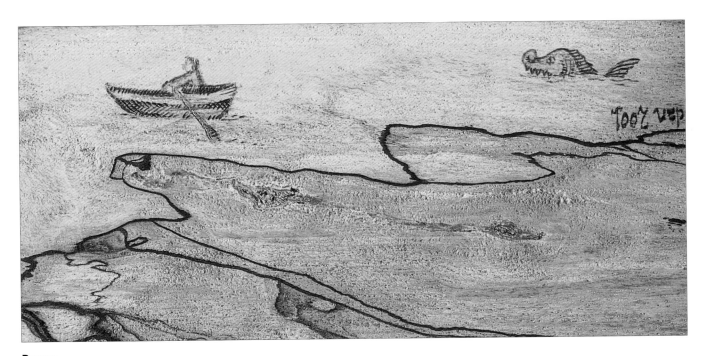

Rower

Human elements add narrative to a piece

Detail of ship

The ships I chose to depict were not necessarily of the same period, but when working with a whimsical subject accuracy, historical or otherwise, is not important.

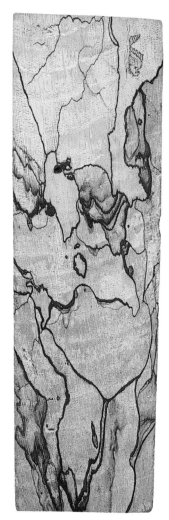

All views

I deliberately kept my design asymmetrical to mimic the asymmetry of the wood. When an effect is designed to be viewed from all angles, you can allow elements of the design to go round corners.

Above and below: the pictorial elements were built up simply using outline and fine cross-hatchings. Sea creatures like these can be found on old maps.

Below: the nautical theme was extended by the inclusion of a compass.

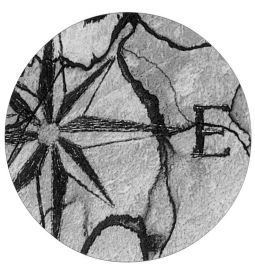

This view shows how little pyrography I actually had to do. When you work on such an interesting canvas the wood can do most of the work for you.

Gourds

I recently discovered the potential of gourds as a suitable canvas for pyrography. A friend of mine once owned an African gourd decorated with animals and patterns. After she lost it, she decided to grow a crop of gourds, presumably in the hope that I could burn her a replacement.

Gourds come in a variety of shapes and sizes and are closely related to pumpkins, squashes and cucumbers. Most are native to Africa and the Americas. Though the fruit is inedible, they have long been valued in African communities. Dried and hollowed out, they can be used to hold liquids and make a wide range of instruments and utensils. Gourds decorated to sell as souvenirs are burnt using primitive tools and traditional designs.

Gourds are easy to grow and most garden centres sell packs of assorted seeds. These should be planted in early spring, started indoors with plenty of water, then planted out when all danger of frost is past. They make attractive additions to your garden and should be picked in the autumn. Cut them to preserve a length of the stalk, which will make the finished product look more complete.

Irregularly-shaped and bumpy gourds will be unsuitable for pyrography, so avoid the labour of drying and scraping these. All others should be left to dry out naturally, in damp-free conditions, for up to a year. The longer you leave the gourds before removing the skin, the more brittle it becomes, and the easier to scrape off. To speed up the drying process, you may wish to scrape off the skin at an early stage. This allows the fleshy middle of the gourd to evaporate more easily.

Your prepared gourds will be strong with a look and feel resembling turned wood. Some may contain seeds and will rattle when shaken. Gourds, at their best, will take the very finest detail that pyrography can produce. You should reserve very smooth gourds for your most complicated designs. Most gourds, however, will have many bumps and irregularities. I treat these gourds with more caution, and either try to avoid the more difficult areas, or stick to designs with very dark worked areas, allowing the opportunity to simply block in stains and imperfections.

When working on a gourd, first remove the stalk at its base. This makes the decorating process easier, and the stalk can be replaced afterwards with a spot of strong wood glue.

Japanese Finch gourd

This design was inspired by oriental porcelain. Gourds offer certain advantages over wood. There is no grain to be considered so you can include extra detail, but natural variations in colour add interest to the background.

Decorated gourds

*The best gourds afford a comprehensive range
of tones while others may burn very unevenly.
The range of design and level of difficulty
shown in this bowl of finished examples reflects
the suitability of gourds for pyrography.*

Preparing the gourd

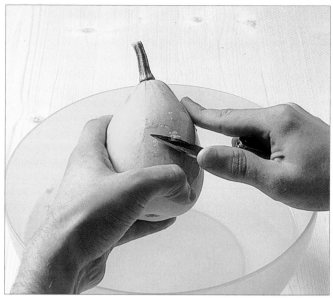

1. Submerge the gourd in hot water for about ten minutes to soften the skin.

2. With a sharp knife and scraping away from yourself, remove the skin. This should come away from the core just as bark lifts from trees, without damaging the surface. Further soaking in hot water may be required. Leave to dry thoroughly before use.

Natural gourds

A wide range of gourds can be grown. Where possible, select smooth, even examples for pyrography work.

Dream gourd

This reverse silhouette illustration is reminiscent of Indian dream pictures. On uneven gourds, troublesome areas are easier to work if you use only very dark pyrography.

My reference sketch

Leather

Leather is a popular medium with pyrographers, and some choose to work only on leather. This is due to the crispness of line that is produced, and no doubt, the immediacy of burning. Since leather burns faster than wood, the surface is covered more quickly.

When working on leather, less heat is generally required. Too much heat will cause overburn (an unsightly orange scorch that can be left around your lines), much the same as on fast-burning woods. It can be slightly unpredictable: it may appear smooth and consistent, but can burn randomly faster or slower. Use less heat and work more slowly for better results. Use a very soft pencil to draw your designs on the leather: it will not show up very well, but it will at least give you a guide.

Working in mid-tones is very difficult on leather, especially on the soft leather usually produced for pyrography. For this reason, it is best to work in simple dark line, using either silhouette techniques, borders or decorative motifs. Celtic designs work especially well as the crisp lines contrast with the colours of the leather.

Leather products such as bookmarks, bracelets and purses are inexpensive and readily available from pyrography suppliers. These are light in colour and well suited to the job. Other items, such as dog collars, suitcases or even leather jackets may prove suitable.

The smell of burning leather is not very pleasant, so if you plan to work with it for long periods make sure the room you are working in is adequately ventilated.

Leather panel

The design of this piece, shown full size, was taken from a Walter Crane pen-and-ink sketch. It is rarely possible to produce a wide colour range comfortably on leather, but this piece proved exceptional. Hard leathers burn beautifully and allow you more control: I found the leather so receptive that after completing what was initially intended to be a line drawing I decided to add tonal depth. I used the bowl of a spoon-point nib to wash over areas in a painterly manner, much as a watercolourist might add washes over a pen sketch, and was able to produce a variety of colours.

A selection of small leather articles suitable for pyrography projects

INDEX

Sycamore mirror

The elaborate shaped border of this mirror was adapted from a rectangular border inspired by the Arts and Crafts movement.